*S*PORTS GREAT

TIGER WOODS

SPORTS GREAT OSCAR DE LA HOYA
0-7660-1066-X/ Torres

SPORTS GREAT JEFF GORDON
0-7660-1469-X/ Macnow

SPORTS GREAT WAYNE GRETZKY
0-89490-757-3/ Rappoport

SPORTS GREAT KEN GRIFFEY, JR.
0-7660-1266-2/ Savage

SPORTS GREAT GRANT HILL
0-7660-1467-3/ Torres

SPORTS GREAT DEREK JETER
0-7660-1470-3/ Knapp

SPORTS GREAT MICHAEL JORDAN
0-89490-978-9/ Aaseng

SPORTS GREAT REBECCA LOBO
0-7660-1466-5/ Savage

SPORTS GREAT STEPHON MARBURY
0-7660-1265-4/ Savage

SPORTS GREAT JERRY RICE
0-89490-419-1/ Dickey

SPORTS GREAT PETE SAMPRAS
0-89490-756-5/ Sherrow

For Other *Sports Great Titles* call:
(800) 398-2504

TIGER WOODS

Glen Macnow

—SPORTS GREAT BOOKS—

Enslow Publishers, Inc.
40 Industrial Road   PO Box 38
Box 398

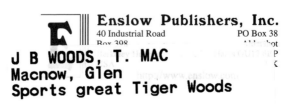

Dedication

To my Parents, Joan and Marvin Macnow,
who taught me everything about hard work, love of family,
and dealing with both success and failure.

Library of Congress Cataloging-in-Publication Data

Macnow, Glen.
    Sports great Tiger Woods / Glen Macnow.
        p. cm. — (Sports great books)
    Includes index.
    ISBN 0-7660-1468-1
        1. Woods, Tiger—Juvenile literature. 2. Golfers—United States—Biography—
Juvenile literature. 3. Racially mixed people—United States—Biography—
Juvenile literature. [1. Woods, Tiger. 2. Golfers. 3. Racially mixed people—
Biography.] I. Title. II. Series.
    GV964.M33   2001
    796.352'092—dc21

                                                    00-010754

Printed in the United States of America

10 9 8 7 6 5 4 3 2 1

To Our Readers: We have done our best to make sure all Internet addresses in this book
were active and appropriate when we went to press. However, the author and the pub-
lisher have no control over and assume no liability for the material available on those
Internet sites or on other Web sites they may link to. Any comments or suggestions can
be sent by e-mail to comments@enslow.com or to the address on the back cover.

Illustration Credits: AP/Wide World Photos

Cover Illustration: AP/Wide World Photos

Contents

Chapter 1

The Young Master

Tiger Woods took a deep breath. He jabbed a golf tee into the green grass.

Standing at the final hole of the 1997 Masters Tournament, Woods knew he had a chance to make history. He stared down the eighteenth fairway of the Augusta National Golf Club and rubbed his hands together. In his mind, he realized what he had to do. If he could cover the 405-yard hole in four strokes, if he could go from tee to hole, he would set an all-time record. He would shoot the lowest seventy-two-hole total ever in the sixty-one-year history of golf's most important tournament.

Woods hiked up the left sleeve of his red golf shirt. He drew back his golf club. Just as he started uncoiling his drive, a camera—one of hundreds focused on him—clicked loudly. Caught off guard, he jerked his swing. His shot hooked left. It went off the fairway, into a patch of azalea bushes.

He looked into the crowd of more than a thousand people, all packed in to watch him play. He could not find

Tiger tees off on the ninth hole of the second round of Masters play at the Augusta National Golf Club in 1997.

the offending camera. Now he needed to recover. To get the record, he could afford no more bad shots. As he walked toward his ball, Woods thought of the history he was about to make. It would be great for him, but he also wanted to do something for the golfers of color who had come before him. Only three African-American men had ever played this tournament before. So many others had been denied the chance to play by a sport that discriminated against minorities for a century. He closed his eyes and mouthed a few words. "I was saying a little prayer of thanks to all of those guys who helped clear the path for me," he later revealed.

Woods peered over the azaleas, out to the eighteenth green. This would not be an easy shot. He needed to quickly get the ball into the air in order to clear the bushes. He also needed it to land gently, though, without rolling over the green. He took out his wedge; a club with a face lying almost directly on the ground. He took a few practice strokes. Then he smacked the ball with a solid thwack. It quickly rose, covered 140 yards in the air and landed softly, just twelve feet from the hole. The crowd around him went crazy with delight.

Now Woods knew what was about to happen. If he could sink the ball in two putts, he would set the record. He stroked the ball once, and it glided past the hole. He calmly lined up a five-footer and gently tapped it with his putter. It clunked into the hole for a par-4. The record—and The Masters tournament—were his.

Woods threw an uppercut toward the sky in celebration. He hugged his caddy, and then ran off the green to hug his parents, Earl and Kultida Woods. He was crying, but they were tears of joy.

No one had ever seen a performance like this. Woods's four-day score of 270 was 18 strokes under par. It was the lowest Masters score in history. It was also 12 strokes better than any other golfer in the 1997 tournament. No golfer had ever run away with a Masters like that.

Just twenty-one years old, Tiger was the youngest golfer ever to wear the green jacket awarded to The Masters champion. He was the first minority golfer ever to win the tournament. And he did it all in his first year as a professional golfer.

President Clinton called him that night to offer congratulations and ask for some golf tips. Around the country, more people watched The Masters that day than had ever viewed any golf event on television. Woods was the attraction. Woods was the star.

Tiger Woods had changed the face of golf.

* * *

Ask long-time fans to name the greatest golfer of all time, and they will probably argue among Bobby Jones, Ben Hogan, and Jack Nicklaus. Then ask them to predict who will be the greatest golfer of the next twenty-five years. There should be no debate. Everyone agrees it will be the young guy with the graceful swing and the great ability to focus under pressure.

Tiger Woods was famous before he even turned professional. As a little boy, he appeared on national television shows to take on celebrities in putting contests. As a teenager, Tiger entered golf history with the best amateur record of all time. That record included three straight U.S. Junior Amateur championships and three more U.S. Amateur Tournament wins. Amateur contests are those in which the players do not get paid for winning.

Woods became a pro in 1996 when he was just twenty years old. Many so-called experts figured that the young man would have a tough time competing against the world's greatest players. Woods quickly proved the experts wrong. He played in twenty-five tournaments in his first

Tiger Woods celebrates after winning the 1997 Masters golf tournament.

twelve months on the pro tour. He finished first six times. Some good golfers do not win six titles in their entire career. After Woods won The Masters tournament in April 1997, golfer Tom Lehman said, "He threw down the gauntlet and said, 'This is golf in the 21st Century.' Now we all have to chase Tiger."

There is much about Tiger Woods that makes him the buzz of the golf world. First there is his swing. Woods is thin—he stands six feet two inches but weighs just 155 pounds. Despite that build, he owns one of the most powerful drives in the game. His tee shots average nearly 300 yards—the length of three football fields. That makes him especially good on the long par-5 holes—he usually reaches the green in just two shots.

Power is just one of his gifts. Woods is an expert at golf's mind games. He always seems to know when to pull up for a safe shot or when to gamble and go all out for a riskier shot. He has a great ability to block out distractions. That is an essential skill in a sport in which the slightest twitch can ruin a shot. As Woods explained, "My body knows how to play golf. I've trained it to do that. It's just a matter of keeping my conscious mind out of it."

Concentration is something he needs to rely on more and more. Woods draws the biggest and loudest galleries on the pro circuit. Galleries are the crowds that follow golfers from hole to hole as they play the course. At some tournaments, word that Tiger will play has caused ticket sales to double. He has had a giant role in increasing the number of young people and minority-group members who now consider the game of golf to be almost as cool as basketball.

That alone, is a big change. Golf was one of the last sports dominated almost exclusively by whites, and wealthy whites at that. Part of that is due to economics. Golf is an expensive sport. A good set of golf clubs costs hundreds of

The 1997 Masters champion Tiger Woods receives his green jacket from Nick Faldo, the previous year's champ.

dollars, or even more than a thousand. A day on a public golf course can easily cost $50. Membership at a country club can cost more than $10,000 a year. Those costs put golf out of the reach of many aspiring athletes.

Beyond that, the golfing establishment was reluctant to open up to minority people. For decades, African Americans and other minorities were often barred from joining most country clubs. Just a handful of African-American golfers made it to the pro tour before Tiger Woods, and none had great success. So it is not surprising that Woods is often compared to baseball player Jackie Robinson and tennis player Arthur Ashe. Both were African Americans who opened up their sports to minorities.

Like those two superstars, Woods has another great talent. It is one that is hard to put your finger on, one that cannot be measured by statistics. Call it charisma. It is the ability to turn fans on, like Wayne Gretzky did soaring down the ice. It is the ability to create memories, like Michael Jordan making the final shot of his career to win another NBA title. He is even blessed with first-name recognition, the signature of legends—Pele, Magic, Elvis. The fact that his given name is Eldrick Woods does not really matter. By the time he was three, everyone knew him as Tiger. It was a nickname given to him by his dad. It was once the nickname of a heroic South Vietnamese soldier Col. "Tiger" Vuong Dang Phong, who had fought by Earl Woods' side during the Vietnam War and once saved his life.

Earl Woods is one-quarter Chinese, one-quarter American Indian, and one-half African American. Earl's wife, Kultida Woods, is one-half Thai, one-quarter Chinese, and one-quarter white. The two met and married in 1969, when Earl Woods was stationed with the U.S.

Tiger and Earl Woods look over old photos of the late Col. "Tiger" Vuong Dang Phong, whom Tiger Woods is nicknamed after. Sitting opposite them is Phong's son, Vuong Dang Phouc. Tom Callahan and Tida Woods stand in the background.

Army in Thailand. Six years later, Kultida—known to everyone as Tida—gave birth to Tiger, her only child.

The ethnic background actually makes Tiger more Asian than he is African American. Once, he was asked if it bothers him that most people identify him simply as being African American.

"It does," he said. "Growing up, I came up with this name: I'm a 'Cablinasian.' " That, he said, is a term to mix all of his roots: Caucasian, black, American Indian and

Asian. One time, when filling out a form, he was asked to check a box for racial background. He could not settle on just one.

"I checked off 'African American' and 'Asian.' Those are the two I was raised under. But my parents didn't raise me to be a black this or an Asian that. They raised me to be the best person I could be."

In reality, they raised him to be something special.

Chapter 2

A Natural

There is no question that much of Tiger Woods's success comes from his parents. His mother gave him discipline, patience, and self-respect. His father gave him a competitive drive and a love for the sport of golf.

Earl Woods was an excellent baseball catcher in college. He gave up sports when he joined the military. But he never gave up his love of the games. Earl Woods took up golf at the age of forty-two, just two years before Tiger was born. Like so many golfers, he became addicted to the sport. He would practice his stroke hour after hour, knocking plastic balls into a net he set up in the garage. When Tiger was about six months old, Earl Woods would carry the baby into the garage, strap him in his high chair, and practice his swings while the infant watched in awe.

Tiger watched for four months. Then, when he was ten months old, he climbed down from the high chair. Though he could barely walk, he picked up a plastic putter. He eyed the ball. He swung, and the ball sailed right into the net. Earl Woods could not believe it.

"I knew then and there he was something special," Earl said. "And I knew golf would be perfect for my son. I wanted to give him a game for a lifetime."

Tiger Woods owes much of his success to his parents, Earl and Tida Woods. They taught him the values of patience, respect, and hard work.

Earl Woods devised a plan. He would give Tiger every chance to develop his talent, but never force him to play or practice. If Tiger was to succeed at the game, he had to love golf for himself.

There was no doubt that Tiger did love golf. By the age of eighteen months, he was spending his days putting on the practice green and hitting tee shots at a nearby driving range. When he was done hitting, his mother would put him back in the stroller, and he would fall asleep. While other toddlers played in sandboxes, Tiger practiced chipping out of sand traps.

"When he was two years old, he memorized my work number," said Earl Woods. "He would call me every day and ask if we could play golf together. When I would agree he was so excited."

That same year, Tiger won his first tournament, wearing diapers. He used sawed-off clubs, since regular ones were taller than he was. At age three, he was invited to appear on *The Mike Douglas Show*, a national television show. There, he beat movie stars Bob Hope and Jimmy Stewart—both avid golfers—in a putting contest.

He was a quick learner. At age three, Tiger was able to look at the fourteen clubs in his golf bag and pick the right one for any shot. He shot a 48 over nine holes. All-time great Jack Nicklaus did not accomplish that feat until he was eleven. Some golfers never do that in their lifetimes.

The achievements kept coming. When he was four, Tiger had a pro coach. At the age of five he was asked for his autograph. By the time he was six he had shot his first hole in one.

Life was not all a breeze. Some neighbors in the Woods's town of Cypress, California, disliked having a multi-racial family in the area. They pelted the house with fruit and broke the front window. When Tiger entered

Tiger had a pro coach by the age of four. By the age of six, he had shot his first hole in one.

kindergarten, he learned that some people would mistreat him because of his racial makeup. Walking home from school, he was grabbed by some older boys. They tied him to a tree and threw rocks at him. For weeks afterward, he was afraid to go back to school.

There was prejudice on the golf course as well. Earl Woods had heard racial slurs when he started playing at the Navy Golf Course, a private club, in 1975. When Tiger started joining him, some club members mumbled that children should be barred. That seemed strange to Earl Woods. He had seen children there for years and no one had ever complained before. Now Tiger was asked to leave.

So Earl Woods came up with a challenge. Six-year-old Tiger would take on the club's teaching pro. If Tiger won, no one could ever again ask him to leave the course. But if the pro won, Tiger and his dad would go away forever. The match took place, and Tiger, unbelievably, won by two strokes.

Still, when other club members heard about the match, they claimed the club pro had no right to accept the challenge. They voted Tiger and his dad out of the private course. The Woods' moved their game to Heartwell Park, a public course in nearby Long Beach. Although Earl Woods was upset about the move, he decided to make the best of it. He noticed that Heartwell Park was a shorter course with tricky holes. So he taught Tiger to focus on his short game—approach shots, chip shots, and difficult shots out of sand traps. In all, it made Tiger a better player.

By the time Tiger was seven, Earl Woods knew his son had the talent to become a great professional golfer. He also knew that many talented people never reach their goals. So Earl Woods did everything he could to make Tiger not just a better player but a tougher player as well. He brought home tapes with subliminal—or hidden—messages.

Underneath the soothing music or sounds of running water were messages such as "I believe in me." The tapes were supposed to give Tiger confidence.

Earl Woods also tried to prepare his son for the day when he would have to make shots in front of rowdy crowds. On the course, Earl Woods would wait for Tiger to line up his shot. Then he would jangle the coins in his pocket or drop a ball directly in Tiger's path. While it seemed that the father was just trying to irritate his son, he was really doing much more. If Tiger could learn to ignore these annoyances, he would become a much tougher golfer.

Once, after a bad shot in a junior tournament, Tiger smashed his club on his bag in frustration. Tida Woods saw her son lose his cool. She reported him to the tournament director and demanded that Tiger be penalized two strokes. She hurt her son's chances that day because she wanted to make him better in the long run. Another time, when Tiger and his mom were watching television, they saw tennis star John McEnroe start tossing his racquet around in anger. "Do you see that?" Mrs. Woods asked. "Never behave that way. I will spank you in a moment if you do that. I don't want you to ruin my reputation as a parent."

Everything was geared toward making Tiger into a champion. Earl Woods spent thousands of dollars on equipment. He hired the best coaches. He even quit his job to devote all of his time to his talented young son. By age eleven, Tiger had played in thirty tournaments, winning every one.

Still, there was time for fun. "I had a normal childhood," Tiger said. "I did the same things every kid did. I studied and went to the mall. I was addicted to TV wrestling, rap music and *The Simpsons*. I got into trouble and got out of it. I loved my parents and obeyed what they

Tiger had already played in thirty tournaments by the time he was eleven years old. He won every one of them.

told me. The only difference is that I can sometimes hit a little ball into a hole in less strokes than some other people."

By the time Tiger was thirteen, it was clear that golf was his future. As a teen, he entered tournaments from Texas to Florida to New York. He usually won. He played with every golfer from Sam Snead to Jack Nicklaus to Greg Norman. Golfing legend Byron Nelson played a round with Tiger just before the boy turned fourteen. "I've seen Ben Hogan and Jack Nicklaus and Tom Watson," Nelson said afterward. "I've seen them all. This fellow has no weakness."

Tiger tried other sports. He was a natural switch-hitter in baseball, a decent shooting guard in basketball, and a good 400-yard runner in track. He quit them all, though, because they interfered with golf.

By 1991, Tiger was ready for the big time. He entered the U.S. Junior Championship in Orlando, Florida. The tournament was open to players seventeen years old and under. Tiger was just fifteen. On the final day, with just twelve holes remaining, he trailed the leader by three strokes. That is a lot to make up in less than one round. Many golfers would have folded, but Tiger staged a comeback. By the end of the round, he had pulled into a tie for first place. A playoff was held to decide the winner. Tiger won it on the first hole, celebrating with an uppercut punch into the air that would later become his trademark. He became the youngest golfer ever to win the Junior Amateur.

He won that same tournament the next year. Also in 1992, Tiger was invited to play in the Los Angeles Open, making him the youngest player ever to take part in an official Professional Golfers Association (PGA) tournament. Unlike the other players—all grown men—he needed to get permission from his school to appear on the course.

Life was great for this high school student. At age

Tiger hugs his father, Earl, during a press conference in 1997. Earl Woods devoted much of his life to making Tiger a champion.

seventeen, he had a girlfriend and a car. He was getting As and Bs in school. He was beating golfers his age and competing against the best in the world.

Then it all caught up to him. Tiger was running so hard that he did not have time to rest. He would skip a meal and then eat seven slices of pizza later to make up for it. The lifestyle wore him down. He came down with mononucleosis, a virus that left him so weak and tired that he could not pick up a club. A doctor gave him orders—for two months he had to stay in bed.

For a while, at least, he was off the tour.

Chapter 3

Amateur Career

The mononucleosis virus sidelined Tiger Woods through the spring of 1993. When he finally picked up his clubs again, he was weak and rusty. He wanted to get back to form in time for the U.S. Junior Championship in August. He had won it the two previous years. No one had ever taken that tournament three years in a row.

Tiger made it to the tournament in Portland, Oregon, but his weariness showed. Going into the final day, he trailed the leader by five strokes. That morning, he ate breakfast by himself and went for a walk. He asked himself questions: How much did he want to win? Did he have what it took to overcome hard times? A true champion, he told himself, would not let this illness stop him.

Tiger played one of the best rounds of his life. After seventeen holes, he had made up four strokes. He was down by one going into the final hole. It was a tough par-5, meaning that a good golfer would need five strokes to go from tee to hole. Tiger slammed a three hundred-yard drive. He then slapped a shot into the sand. His third shot landed on the green, ten feet from the hole. That is no easy putt, but Tiger put it down, to tie the contest at the end of regulation.

Now he was on his game. On the very first playoff hole, Tiger sank a twenty-foot putt to take the title. The gallery went wild. They knew that the teenager with the sweet stroke and winning grin would some day take his game to the pros.

First Tiger would choose a college. Woods was offered an athletic scholarship to Stanford University in 1994. Some golf fans thought he was wasting his time at the Palo Alto, California, college and should go professional immediately. Tiger's parents were leading him in a different direction.

Tiger Woods fights his way free from a sand trap. Tiger is the only player to win three U. S. Junior Championships in a row.

"I want you to finish school," Earl Woods told his son. "Jack Nicklaus did not finish school. Arnold Palmer did not finish school. Curtis Strange did not finish school. But you can do everything."

Tiger heard his father. "I promise you, Dad," he said.

In fact, Tiger loved college. Although the courses were tough, he did well. He joined the Sigma Chi fraternity. He went to parties, although his athletic skills did not help him on the dance floor. Said his classmate, Mark Poe, "Tiger Woods is maybe the greatest golfer of all time, but he is probably the worst dancer." He made friends. Some were quite famous, such as actor Fred Savage of the TV show *The Wonder Years*, Olympic gymnast Dominique Dawes, and Kristin Folke, the captain of Stanford's national champion women's volleyball team.

"I'm not a celebrity at Stanford," Tiger said. "Everybody's special. You have to be to get in here. So then nobody is. That's why I love the place."

Certainly his mates on the golf team did not treat him as special. As a freshman, he was made to carry the extra luggage on road trips. When he took out his contact lenses and put on glasses, his teammates cracked up. They nicknamed him Urkel, after the goofy television character.

Still, not everyone appreciated him. Soon after arriving at Stanford, Tiger received an anonymous letter. It attacked his ethnic heritage and threatened his life if he stayed at college.

Tiger showed the letter to a teammate. "Look at this," he said. "I'm not going to forget about this." He taped the letter to the wall of his dorm room as a reminder of what he still faced.

On the golf course, he was better than ever. He staged a dramatic comeback in the 1994 U.S. Amateur Tournament. Unlike most tournaments, this one was match play, meaning that two golfers played each other. The winner went on to the next round. Tiger got to the finals, where he faced Oklahoma State's Trip Kuehne in a grueling thirty-six-hole match.

Kuehne built up a five-stroke lead with just twelve holes to go. Tiger had produced big finishes before, but this one might be impossible. When the match broke for lunch, he showered and changed his clothes. That gave him the feeling he was making a new start.

And start again he did. Tiger made up those five strokes over the next ten holes. With just two left, he and Kuehne were even.

The next hole was a dangerous one. Nicknamed the Island Hole, it had a green completely surrounded by water. A bad shot here would put the ball smack into the pond. Many golfers take a safe route—hitting to the end of the fairway and then lobbing a short chip shot over the water onto the green. That is what Kuehne did, getting onto the green in two strokes.

Tiger knew this was no time to play it safe. He went for broke with a shot that even the top pros rarely try. He took out his nine iron and aimed to hit the ball all the way to the green in just one stroke. If he made it, he would have a chance for a birdie—and the win. If he did not, he would lose the tournament.

Knowing what Tiger was planning, the crowd grew silent. With his perfect sweet stroke, Tiger lofted a shot that flew high over the water. It came down, took one hop on the green, and stopped rolling, barely three feet from the water. As the fans cheered their approval, Tiger calmly curled a fourteen-foot putt into the hole. He celebrated the win with his trademark uppercut into the air.

Amateurs do not receive money for tournament wins, but Tiger won something else. By taking the Amateur, he won an invitation to the 1995 Masters tournament. That is

Tiger proudly holds up the U.S. Amateur Golf Championship trophy. Tiger won the Amateur championship three straight years, from 1994 through 1996.

golf's biggest event. It draws the world's greatest pros. And it draws media attention from around the world.

Tiger was so excited he could barely contain himself. For months before the April event, he studied videotapes of previous Masters. He wanted to get a feel for the tournament as best as he could. He learned that the greens at the Augusta National course were hard and slick. So he set up a putting green on the hardwood floor at Maples Pavilion, Stanford's basketball arena. His carpeted dorm room was not smooth enough.

In April, Tiger's dad took him to Georgia for the big event. Earl Woods dropped his son off at his hotel and, as an afterthought, asked how Tiger was fixed for cash. Tiger opened his wallet. It contained five dollars. Here he was, in the lap of luxury and among some of the world's wealthiest men, and Tiger had not brought enough to buy lunch.

On the course, he had no problems. In the days leading up to The Masters, the skinny teenager played practice rounds with some of the greats. He easily held his own. Australia's Greg Norman spent an afternoon with Tiger and was asked afterward what would represent a good weekend for the kid.

"Probably for him, to win," Norman said. "He is good enough."

Tiger did not win, but he did well enough. He shot a 72 the first day—four strokes better than what Jack Nicklaus or Arnold Palmer shot their first time out at Augusta. In the end he finished in forty-first place. He did not embarrass himself, but he knew he could do better. He was nervous and wound up hitting the ball too long. Besides that, he was the only Masters player who had to read a history text book at night following a long day of work. Right after the tourney, he had to return to Stanford for a final exam.

Tiger had other strong feelings about The Masters. The

Tiger tees off during a practice round before the 1995 Masters Tournament while Ray Floyd (left) and Greg Norman (center) look on. Tiger's Amateur Championship earned him a trip to The Masters that year.

greatest golfers had won there, taking the green jacket that is awarded instead of a trophy. It was truly an event for champions. Yet for years, it had been closed to men of color. Tiger knew that African Americans had been welcome on the course only recently. Tiger was the first black amateur to play The Masters. In sixty-one years, only three other African-American golfers had played the links. The club itself admitted no African American members until 1990. Now here he stood in the locker room.

If being a trail blazer came with the territory, Tiger was ready.

Tiger won the U.S. Amateur championship in 1995 and again in 1996. He was the first player since the legendary

Bobby Jones to win a national title six years in a row. As a junior, he was named College Golfer of the Year. He spent hours—usually by himself—practicing at the driving range and on the putting green. He also spent time in the weight room, adding muscle to his thin frame.

The life was a strain. If Tiger dedicated the needed time to his game, his studies suffered. If he concentrated on schoolwork, he lost an edge on the golf course. Something had to give. Tiger had promised his parents he would finish college, but he did not promise he would finish it in four straight years.

After winning the 1996 U.S. Amateur Tournament, Tiger announced that he was leaving college to go pro. Almost immediately, he landed a $40 million endorsement contract with Nike footwear. A few days later, a $20 million deal followed with the golf equipment company Titleist.

The endorsements—and great media attention—came even though he had never won a professional title. Many players privately wondered whether "Tiger-mania" was just a lot of hype.

Soon enough, they would find out otherwise.

Chapter 4

Tigermania

Hype? Hardly. From the moment Tiger Woods first joined the professional tour on August 28, 1996, he showed that he did not just belong with the big boys. In fact, he was better than just about all of them.

In the most successful golf debut in memory, Tiger posted two wins in his first seven Professional Golfers Association (PGA) starts. Many of golf's top players are happy to win one tournament out of every fifty. What Woods was doing at the age of twenty seemed impossible. In golf, unlike in most sports, players reach their peak late in their thirties. Tiger's accomplishment was comparable to a thirteen-year-old leading major-league baseball in home runs.

Jack Nicklaus is considered by most to be golf's all-time best. The first time Nicklaus saw Tiger play professionally in 1996 he said, "This kid will win more Masters titles than Arnold Palmer and I did combined." That would mean a whopping eleven green jackets.

Some young stars might be put off by such a prediction. Not Tiger. His goal, he said, is to be the best golfer since fifteenth-century Scottish shepherds first smacked a feather-stuffed ball around the Highlands with their crooks.

Tiger Woods shakes the hand of golf legend Jack Nicklaus after receiving the Jack Nicklaus College Player of the Year Award in 1996. Nicklaus predicted that Tiger would win more Masters titles than himself and Arnold Palmer combined.

You can define Tiger Woods by many things he is not. He is not a tantrum waiting to happen. He is not a spoiled athlete who snubs fans. He is not a young burnout candidate who was over-pressured by his parents.

Instead, Tiger Woods is a confident young man. He is nice enough to sign autographs for kids for an hour after a round. He is gracious enough to sponsor clinics for inner-city kids who think of golf as a miniature course with windmills.

His first tee shot as a pro came on September 1, 1996, at the Greater Milwaukee Open. He drew more attention from fans and reporters than the other 155 players combined. Fans perceived him as being talented, handsome, and charming. And he is a minority athlete in a sport that was (and still is) virtually all white. What golf needed more than anything was a star to shred it of its restrictive image. Here came Tiger.

Tiger did not like the idea of being a role model just for minorities. "I don't consider myself a great black hope," he said. "I'm just a golfer who happens to be black and Asian. It doesn't matter whether anyone is white, black, brown, or green. All that matters is I touch kids the way I can though clinics and they benefit through them."

The Greater Milwaukee Open is normally a small stop on the PGA tour. Thanks to Tiger's pro debut, however, it became a giant event. The television network ESPN decided at the last minute to show the open, adding an extra camera crew just to stay with Woods. Attendance tripled and fans hung outside Tiger's hotel, hoping to see him come or go. For many players, that would be a lot of pressure, but Woods was used to the attention. He finished in sixtieth place—not great, but not bad either. His best moment came when he knocked in a hole-in-one on the final day. He then scooped the ball from the hole and tossed it to an adoring young fan.

His big breakthrough came six weeks later at the Las Vegas Invitational. This tournament drew a tough field of the world's best players. It was a four-round tournament, and Tiger improved his play each round. On the third day, he was limping because of a pulled leg muscle. The pain, he said, just made him more determined.

Beginning the fourth and final day, Tiger was four strokes behind leader Davis Love III. Love was no rookie likely to fold under pressure. He was an experienced professional who had won pro tourneys before. Love shot a solid 1-under-par 71 in his fourth round.

Tiger laughs along with his mother, Tida. Tiger can always count on his mom to be there for emotional support when he needs it.

Tiger chased the leader all day. He shot a 5-under-par 67, and tied Love at the end of regulation. That meant the two men would play a sudden-death match. They would play each other until one got a better score on a particular hole.

This was the first time as a pro that Tiger was in a pressure-packed playoff. He went to the putting green and calmly knocked down a few shots. He ate a banana for energy. He shared a laugh with his father. Then, he went to face down Love.

The first playoff hole was a 380-yarder. Tiger took out his biggest club—his driver. He whacked the ball 330 yards straight down the fairway. Then he took a pitching wedge. He spun a shot that landed eight feet from the flag marking the hole. As Love watched helplessly, Tiger took out his putter. He put his head down and took a few practice swings into the air. He straightened his legs, tapped the ball, and watched it roll straight into the hole. His three strokes gave him a birdie, meaning one under par. The best Love could do was a four. That quickly, the sudden death was over.

As fans screamed his name, Tiger shook hands with his opponent. He collected the winner's check of $175,000. That night he celebrated his first pro victory with a special dinner—two Big Macs at McDonald's.

His second win came just three weeks later, at the Disney World Classic in Orlando, Florida. Fittingly, his winner's check was presented by the *Winnie the Pooh* character of Tigger.

From the start, Tiger Woods said his success came from the help of his parents. His mother, Tida Woods, was his emotional support. She was the person he could go to when he was scared or lonely. Even a twenty-year-old superstar feels scared or lonely once in a while.

His father, Earl Woods, was the man Tiger would go to

for help with major decisions. Earl Woods traveled with his son during Tiger's rookie year on the PGA Tour. He booked hotel rooms, scheduled interviews, and took care of time-consuming errands. Certainly, it let Tiger focus on his job—golfing. But neither man noticed that it might be too much stress for Earl, a man in his sixties. Soon after the Disney World Classic, Earl Woods suffered a heart attack. He was rushed to the hospital for surgery. He recovered, but he was told he could no longer walk eighteen holes each day with his talented son.

Tiger felt a bit lonely without his father on the course, but he was anything but alone. Even as a rookie, Tiger attracted all kinds of fans. His galleries were bigger than those of any golfer since Arnold Palmer. His fans included Asians and blacks, Latinos and whites. There were children and old people chanting his name. Many knew almost nothing about the sport. They were turned on by Woods's personality and background. They came to watch him like fans at a rock concert.

Some golfers need silence in order to concentrate. They might be bothered by the noisy fans. But not Tiger. "I think it's great they come out. I think it's neat because you can never lose a ball."

Not that he slices many balls into the woods. From a technical view, Tiger's swing is nearly perfect. Because he is tall and thin, he coils his body into a tightly wound spring. Then the spring explodes, and his club head meets the ball at more than two hundred miles per hour. He is able to pound the ball more than three hundred yards—the length of almost three major-league home runs. On shorter shots, his steady hands and quick shoulders give him the delicate touch to place the ball where he wants it to go.

Tiger is also unfazed by pressure. He has been playing in tournaments since he was a small boy. The bigger the stakes,

Tiger meets "Tigger" after winning the Disney Golf Classic in Lake Buena Vista, Florida, in October, 1996.

the better he played. For a pro, with prizes approaching $500,000, the ability to stare down pressure is a great help.

From the very start, this personality mix made Tiger Woods an advertiser's dream. Sponsors lined up even before his first win on the PGA Tour. Would he endorse their hamburgers? Would he be a spokesman for their restaurant? One company even wanted Tiger to speak on behalf of a line of women's underwear. He turned most of them down, sticking with a small group of companies he believed in. And he insisted on having some control over what his ads said. His first commercial for Nike, for example, focused on his racial background. "There are still at least twenty-three private clubs in this country that would not have me as a member," he said in the ad. "Isn't it time for a change?"

By the end of his rookie season, Woods had taken the golf world by storm. He won two tournaments and finished in the top ten in three others. He attracted young fans to a sport they had previously thought of as being boring. In one golf program aimed at inner-city teens, for example, the number of kids signing up tripled during Tiger's first three months on the tour.

"Tiger has done what no golfer had done in the past— he made golf cool," said John Morrison, director of the Los Angeles Urban Golf Program.

As Tiger entered the 1997 season, he did more than make golf cool. He made it his own private world.

Chapter 5

Sportsman of the Year

The morning broke warm and sunny. The Augusta National Golf Club was flooded in bright light in early April 10, 1997. The Georgia course was also flooded with great golfers. Nick Faldo, a three-time winner of The Masters, was there. So was Germany's Bernhard Langer, who had won it twice. So was Australian Greg Norman, who had never won—but had finished second three times. Dozens of the hardest hitters and craftiest players were on hand.

All eyes, however, were on a tall, skinny twenty-one-year-old with a sweet stroke. Tiger Woods was the youngest player in the field, by years. He was certainly the least experienced. But no one who watched him standing in the sunlight, cranking out 320-yard practice drives that morning, doubted his chances of winning golf's most important contest.

Tiger had warmed up for The Masters by taking the Mercedes Championship in Hawaii. On this April day, though, nothing mattered beyond The Masters. It was not just the $486,000 first-place prize that mattered to Woods. It was everything that he stood for, and everything The Masters had always been about.

For years, this most important tournament represented golf's racist history. African Americans had been barred until Lee Elder broke the color line in 1975, the year Tiger was born. In the two decades since, just two other African-American men had participated. The private country club did not admit a African-American member until 1990. As tournament founder Clifford Roberts once said, "As long as I'm alive, golfers will be white and caddies will be black."

Tiger Woods loosens up on the eighth hole during the final round of The Masters tournament in 1997.

Onto this scene came Tiger Woods. Someone noted that he arrived in Augusta almost fifty years to the day after Jackie Robinson broke major-league baseball's color barrier. Woods often told people that his goal was not to become known as the world's greatest African-American golfer, but rather the world's greatest golfer, period. He was, however, well aware of the significance of playing in this particular event. He was also well aware that, despite his youth, he was considered a favorite to win. The tournament's long holes and slick greens were suited to his game. No one clobbered the ball as far or controlled the speed of his putts better.

From the start of the four-day tournament, the hype was amazing. The Masters drew its largest-ever crowds. Most of the fans walked hole to hole with Tiger. The weekend broadcasts drew the highest-ever TV ratings for golf. All eyes were on this young newcomer.

Was he nervous? "He may be 21," said Tiger's caddie, Mike "Fluff" Cowan. "But he ain't no 21 inside those ropes."

It did not seem like it at first. The Masters, like most golf tournaments, is four eighteen-hole rounds over four days. On the first day, Thursday, Tiger got off to a terrible start. He looked lost and nervous. He made four bad tee shots on the first nine holes and had a score of 40. No man with that bad a start had ever won The Masters.

Then something clicked in his mind. On the tenth hole he shortened his swing. The result was a birdie. His smooth stroke kicked back in. He started making some clutch putts. He shot a 30 for the back nine, giving him 70 for the day. Not a great round, but a good recovery from disaster. He trailed leader John Huston by three strokes.

That night, Woods ate burgers and fries with a friend who had come to keep him company. They played Ping-Pong and a game of one-on-one the basketball court. They screamed and laughed so loudly playing video games that they drove Tiger's parents to the far edge of their rented house. It was not typical behavior for a professional golfer, but it was a great way for a twenty-one-year-old guy to relax under pressure.

Tiger came back for Friday's round feeling invigorated. He shot a 66, the best round of the day. Suddenly, he was in the lead, three strokes ahead of Colin Montgomerie.

On Saturday, he was even better. Tiger did not make a single mistake in one of the most amazing rounds ever seen. As the rest of the field slumped, he shot a 65, tying the course record. By day's end, he was nine shots ahead of everyone—an amazing lead in golf. At the Augusta clubhouse that night, other golfers shook their heads in wonderment. No one debated who would win.

"There is no chance," said Montgomerie. "We're all human beings here. There's no chance humanly possible."

Heading into Sunday's final round, the question was not whether Tiger would win. The question was whether he could break the all-time low score for the tournament. He needed a 3-under-par 69. That certainly seemed possible. After all, he had averaged 67 the first three days.

That morning, a blustery wind flapped the yellow flags that flew over each hole. Woods put on the red shirt he sometimes wears for luck. His biggest concern was losing focus. He knew all eyes would be on him. He knew people expected him to be perfect. The galleries would be noisy, the television cameras confusing. He and his father smiled at each other. They knew the mental toughness from Tiger's childhood would pay off on this day.

Tiger scored a par-4 on the first hole. He got down in three on the second, 1-under par. Then, his game escaped him. On the fifth hole, he cranked a tee shot into the woods, right behind a tree. On the seventh, he buried a ball in a sand trap and needed two strokes to get out. Was the

LEADERS

PRIOR	HOLE	1	2	3	4	5	6	7	8	9	10	11	12	13	14	15	16	17	18
	PAR	4	5	4	3	4	3	4	5	4	4	4	3	5	4	5	3	4	4
15	WOODS	15	16	16	16	15	15	14	15	15	15	16	16	17	18				
6	ROCCA	6	7	7	7	7	6	6	6	6	6	5	5	5	5				
5	STANKOWSKI	5	4	3	2	2	2	3	3	2	3	2	2	2	3	3			
4	KITE T.	4	5	5	4	4	3	4	5	5	5	5	5	6	6	5			
4	WATSON. T.	5	6	6	6	7	6	3	4	4	5	5	6	6	6	6	5		
3	SLUMAN	3	3	3	3	2	2	3	3	3	3	3	3	4	5	3	3		
1	LOVE	0	1	0	0	1	0	0	0	0	0	0	1	3	3	4	3	3	
2	LANGER	2	1	2	2	2	2	1	0	1	0	0	0	1	1	2	2	2	2
2	COUPLES	2	3	3	3	2	1	2	2	2	2	2	2	3	1	1	2	3	
0	TOLLES	0	1	2	2	2	2	2	1	2	2	2	2	3	3	4	5	5	5

Tiger hits from the gallery during the fifteenth hole of the final round of the 1997 Masters.

pressure getting to him? Once again, Woods took a short private walk to calm down. He thought, "Just play like I know how. Pretend I'm all alone on the course. Relax and have fun."

So he did. On the eighth hole, Tiger dropped in a long rolling shot that seemed to set him up for the rest of the afternoon. From that point on, he was close to perfect. When he tapped in his final putt on 18, he was the proud owner of the best Masters score ever. He ended up with an 18-under-par 270.

Tiger tossed his winning ball into the crowd to give them a souvenir. He and caddie Fluff Cowen exchanged high fives. Waiting for his son off the eighteenth green was Earl Woods, still recovering from his earlier heart attack. Father and son embraced in a big bear hug. "It was the first tournament he was able to go to since his surgery," said Tiger. "It was nice to have him back on the team."

Tiger had won the tournament he had talked about winning since age five, the tournament he watched on tape nearly every night in his bedroom, the tournament he wanted more than all the others. He was the youngest man by two years to win The Masters. He was the first minority golfer to win any of golf's four major tournaments.

Someday, this multi-racial man from a middle-class background may be hailed as the greatest golfer who ever lived. It is likely that his finest day will always be the over-cast Sunday in April 1997 when he humiliated the world's greatest golfers. He shot 18-under-par (70-66-65-69-270) and won The Masters easily. It was the soundest whipping in any golf tournament of the century. One of the record audience that watched on television that day was the president of the United States. Bill Clinton, a weekend golfer himself, called to congratulate Tiger Woods.

Tiger was handed his victory check. He was wearing a red shirt and black pants. When he slipped on his green

Tiger Woods embraces Lee Elder after winning the 1997 Masters. Elder was the first African American to play The Masters, doing so in 1975.

Masters jacket, he was wearing the colors of African nationalism. Watching it all, Earl Woods said, "Green and black go well together, don't they?"

When the TV cameras finally turned off and the reporters asked all their questions, Tiger prepared to leave Augusta National. On his way out, he spotted Lee Elder, the first African-American man to play The Masters in 1975. Woods stopped and gave Elder a gentle hug. "Thanks for making this possible," Tiger whispered in his ear. Elder had tears in his eyes.

Tiger finished 1997 as hot as he had started it. He was the favorite at every tournament. If he did not win, he usually came in the top three. At year's end, he was named *Sports Illustrated* Sportsman of the Year. The Associated Press named him the world's most outstanding athlete of the year, ahead of tennis star Pete Sampras, boxer Evander Holyfield, and NFL quarterback Brett Favre.

For Tiger, it was not just what he accomplished in 1997, but what he represented beyond that year. He had changed the face of golf. Young people, minorities, and others who once had no interest in the sport were drawn in by this great new performer. Teens who once wanted to "Be Like Mike," as in Jordan, now wanted to "Catch the Tiger." Never before had one man instantly added so many new fans to a sport.

Tiger's game was so good that no one had ever seen anything like it. His drives off the tee routinely went twenty yards farther than anyone else's, and, they always seemed to travel straight down the fairway. His short shots were gentle and accurate. His putts seemed to fall in from any distance.

Here was the scary part: The day before 1997 ended, Tiger celebrated his twenty-second birthday. If there was one thing everyone agreed on, it was this: He was only going to get better.

Chapter 6

Being the Best

S*wish. . . boom! Swish . . . boom! Swish . . . boom!*

It is seven in the morning. The sun has barely risen, but Tiger Woods is already grooving his swing on the practice range. It is the one place he can find an escape from being the most recognizable star in sports since Michael Jordan.

Tiger hits about eight hundred balls nearly every morning. He switches clubs every hundred shots or so, trying to fine-tune every part of his game. Then he works on his putting for up to four hours.

It is not easy to stay on top. Golf may be the toughest of all sports to dominate because there are so many good players on the PGA Tour. On any given week, as many as fifty players have a real shot to win an event.

Tiger does not want to be just another guy with a shot to win. "He has an inward desire to be the best player the planet has ever seen," said Butch Harmon, who has been Tiger's coach since 1992. "So he has made himself incredibly strong for a golfer—both mentally and physically."

That means getting up before dawn to whack bucket after bucket of balls. It means daily fitness training at the weight machines. In the past few years, Tiger built himself into a strong athlete with a broad back and well-defined arms. Every day he bench presses 225 pounds and squats more than three hundred.

It is all part of being the most watched player on the PGA Tour, and it is something Tiger had to learn for himself. His Masters win at age twenty-one had many calling him the sport's best ever. Sometimes, when success comes too early and too easy, it is tough to stay on top.

For a while, Tiger struggled a bit. After winning six PGA events in his first ten months as a pro, he won just two in the next twenty-two months. He found that fame may have done wonderful things for his bank account, but it did not help his golf game. The constant crush of fans, reporters, and promoters cut into his practice time. He became erratic at driving and at putting. By early 1999,

Tiger Woods lines up a putt during the Williams World Challenge at the Grayhawk Golf Club in Scottsdale, Arizona, in December, 1999.

some wondered whether Tiger Woods would be a shooting star who shone for a brief moment and then disappeared.

Tiger Woods feared that himself. His goal was to be the most dominant golfer in history. So, in the middle of 1999, he changed his game.

First, he taught himself to say no. Tiger had always been available to everyone. Before the 1999 Masters, however, he turned down interviews. He turned away lawyers seeking his name for endorsement deals. He turned away friends eager to crank up the PlayStation. He even turned off his cell phone. Before each tournament, he spent time alone. Sometimes he would just sit by himself. He would go through the golf course hole by hole, visualizing what he would do with each shot.

Tiger also retooled his swing in 1999. He had always hit it farther than anyone else, but control had become a problem. So he and Coach Harmon spent hour after hour, day after day, tinkering with Tiger's form.

The hard work paid off. By year's end, he had put together one of the sport's most dominant seasons in the twentieth century. He won nine of his last thirteen tournaments and earned $6.6 million. No golfer had won as many events in a year since Johnny Miller in 1974. And no golfer had ever won as much prize money.

On December 30, 1999—his twenty-fourth birthday—Tiger was named the Associated Press Male Athlete of the Year for the second time. He was chosen over cyclist Lance Armstrong and Boston Red Sox pitcher Pedro Martinez.

The turnaround started in August at the PGA Championship in Medinah, Illinois. Tiger had taken a few weeks off the tour to prepare for this event. It is one of golf's four major tournaments, just like The Masters. It was one he really wanted to win.

Tiger quickly snatched the lead. After three rounds, he was two shots ahead of Sergio Garcia, a nineteen-year-old

Tiger swings away during the Johnnie Walker Classic golf tournament in Taiwan in November, 1999.

surprise from Spain. As they began the final round on Sunday, Tiger wondered whether he could stay ahead of his rival. It was the first time he had played someone younger than he was for a title.

His round started great. Woods came out with four birdies in the first eleven holes. He built his lead up to five strokes. Yet Garcia kept fighting back. After sixteen holes, Tiger's lead was down to one stroke.

For a very brief moment, Tiger doubted himself. He had never choked under pressure before. Would this be the moment? It did not help that, for the first time in his life, he saw the crowd rooting against him and for his younger opponent.

"I know when I got to seventeen, I had to play the two best holes of my life," Tiger said later. "Despite everything that had happened, I still had the lead. I was completely focused on doing whatever I had to do to keep it."

The seventeenth hole at Medinah is a steeply downhill par-3. It is 212 yards long, mostly over water. Garcia finished the hole in three, meaning that Tiger needed par to keep his lead. Woods misjudged the swirling winds. He jacked a 6 iron over the green and into a gnarled clump of long Kentucky bluegrass.

On his next shot, Tiger muffed a chip shot. He knocked it eight feet from the hole, but it was eight feet straight uphill. For any golfer, the toughest shot is a downhill putt. Miss it and your ball can roll well past the cup, even off the green.

Tiger concentrated. He studied the putt for minutes. He looked at the curve of the green and thought about where it might take his ball. He judged the speed of the green, and how hard he would have to hit his ball. Then he pulled off his golf glove, stood over the ball, and tapped it. It rolled right and then left, dipping into the left corner of the cup. It was as if Tiger had willed it in. It gave him par for the hole—one of the toughest pars he had ever made—and kept his one-stroke lead intact. An easier par on the eighteenth hole iced the championship.

"That putt [on 17] was what all those hours of practice are about," said Tiger. "You need to be able to execute the shots when you absolutely have to."

The win at Medinah was Tiger's second in a PGA major. As a boy, he kept a poster listing all of Jack Nicklaus's major championships tacked up next to his bed. Nicklaus—known as the Golden Bear—won 19 majors during his long career. Tiger's goal has always been to reach that number.

"Tiger wants to be the greatest player ever, and to do that, he knows he has to beat Jack Nicklaus," said Harmon. "Tiger judges all his accomplishments against Jack's."

So it means a lot when Nicklaus himself predicts that Tiger will someday reach his goals.

"He had a phenomenal year," Nicklaus said late in 1999. "I think he has got phenomenal focus. If he can keep that going for a long period of time, he'll break all of my records—and everyone else's."

Tiger won five of his final six PGA Tour events in 1999. He took the final four, for the best streak since Ben Hogan won four straight tour events in 1953.

If that was phenomenal, what Tiger did next was unbelievable. A new streak started in June of 2000. Tiger won the U.S. Open in Pebble Beach, California. That tournament is considered another of golf's four major tournaments. Tiger obliterated the field of 155 competitors. His closest foe, Ernie Els, finished a whopping 15 strokes back. "I played my best," Els said afterward. "But I didn't even belong on the same course as that guy."

Els joked afterward that Tiger might win all four majors in a row. At least it seemed like a joke. No golfer had accomplished a Grand Slam since Bobby Jones in

1930. Back then, two of the four major tournaments were amateur events that drew less competition.

Since the four current majors were set up in the 1940s, only Hogan had won as many as three in a row.

Could Tiger take four straight? People started paying more attention when he captured the British Open in July 2000. That made it two in a row. It also gave him lifetime wins in all four majors. Only a handful of golfers had ever done that—and only Tiger had done so before his twenty-fifth birthday.

Next came the PGA Championship in Louisville, Kentucky. Tiger came in as defending champion. The pressure to repeat was huge, as were the noisy crowds that surrounded Tiger on each shot. But if Tiger felt the pressure, he did not show it. For the better part of four rounds he chased Bob May, a relative unknown. Midway through the final round, he trailed May by three strokes. Then, in the final nine holes, Tiger again took over. He shot a blazing five-under-par 31 in those nine holes. He drained one heroic putt after another. When the scores were counted, Tiger beat May by one stroke.

"This was a very memorable battle today," Tiger said afterward. "It was one of my toughest challenges But you just have to understand what your goal is. I've done it since I was a little boy. I didn't try any harder. I just hit good shots."

If that sounds too easy, understand this: What separates Tiger Woods from other great golfers is not just his skills on the course. It is also his ability to relax under pressure.

Nowhere was that pressure more intense than at the Augusta, Georgia in April 2001. Tiger had made his mark by winning the 1997 Masters Tournament. Now he was back at age twenty-five, trying to string together four major championships in a row.

All eyes were on the young champion. The crowds even followed him to the practice range, where he pounded balls into the twilight after every round, always wanting to stay razor sharp. Tiger started the four-round tournament slowly, shooting a 70 on Thursday, the first day. That wasn't good enough to get him on the leader board, but he didn't seem to mind.

He shot a blazing 66 on Friday, and a 68 on Saturday. When the final round started on Sunday, two men—David Duval and Phil Mickelson—were in striking distance. That morning, Mickelson told reporters that he had no fear of Tiger. "I know how to play under pressure a little bit myself," he said.

But, of course, Mickelson was only fooling himself. On the big-money days (the Masters' top prize is $1 million), no one deals with pressure like Tiger Woods. As Mickelson and Duval tried to catch him, Tiger made clutch shot after clutch shot. Woods hit a daring approach from 149 yards into the perilous 11th hole. The ball grazed the cup for a tap-in birdie, giving Woods a lead that he never let go.

In the end, Tiger holed a 17-foot putt on the eighteenth hole as his opponents watched helplessly. Then he quietly walked off the green, slipping his cap low to cover his tears of joy. He walked into the arms of his father, Earl, who trained him to be a champion, and his mother, Kultida. Four years earlier, Woods exploded on to the golf scene with his remarkable victory at the 1997 Masters. Now he had come full circle.

"I guess I was a little young, a little naive," Woods said, reflecting on that first Masters win. "I didn't understand what I accomplished for at least a year or two after that event. This year, I understand. I have a better appreciation for winning a major championship. To win four of them in succession, it's hard to believe, really."

"I don't know what you would compare it to because

Tiger Woods receives the green winner's jacket from Vijay Singh after winning his second Masters tournament on April 8, 2001. His 2001 Masters victory was also his fourth consecutive major championship.

I'm not so sure there's something you could compare with . . . in modern golf," David Duval observed.

"I've had some special things happen to me," Woods said. "But to win four consecutive majors . . . I don't think I've ever accomplished anything this great."

As he slipped on the champion's green jacket, Tiger said his biggest hope was that his success would encourage young people to take up the sport of golf. And that may prove to be the greatest legacy of Tiger Woods: He added excitement and a new breed of fans to a sport that was considered dull for young people and closed to those of color. He is a pioneer in a sport that long called out for one. At a very young age, he has changed the face of golf.

With talent, charm, and ambition, Tiger Woods also changed the idea of what is possible in his sport. Like

Nicklaus in his prime, he is not playing for money. He is playing for a place in history.

When Michael Jordan retired from the National Basketball Association in 1999, he was asked whether another player in that sport might someday dominate as he had. Not in basketball, Jordan said. But if any athlete alive had a chance to break all the records, he added, it was clearly Tiger Woods.

Tiger does not run from that kind of prediction. In fact, he says, if he can use his fame to assist others, that is fine with him.

"Golf is basically a vehicle for me to help people," he said. "I can inspire lives in a positive way. As long as I can touch one person, I feel I've done my job. But I'm definitely going to try to do a whole lot more than that."

Career Statistics
PGA Tournament Wins

YEAR	TOURNAMENT	+/- PAR	EARNINGS
1996	Las Vegas Invitational	-28	$297,000
1996	Walt Disney World Classic	-21	$216,000
1997	Mercedes Championships	-14	$216,000
1997	The Masters	-18	$486,000
1997	Byron Nelson Classic	-17	$324,000
1998	Bell South Classic	-17	$324,000
1999	Buick Invitational	-22	$486,000
1999	The Memorial	-15	$459,000
1999	Western Open	-15	$450,000
1999	PGA Championship	-11	$630,000
1999	WGC-NEC Invitational	-10	$1,000,000
1999	National Car Rental Classic	-17	$450,000
1999	Tour Championship	-15	$900,000
1999	WGC-American Express Championship	-6	$1,000,000
2000	Mercedes Championships	-16	$522,000
2000	Pebble Beach Pro-Am	-15	$720,000
2000	Bay Hill Invitational	-18	$540,000
2000	Memorial Tournament	-19	$558,000
2000	U.S. Open	-12	$800,000
2000	British Open	-19	$759,150
2000	PGA Championship	-18	$900,000
2000	WGC-NEC Invitational	-21	$1,000,000
2000	Canadian Open	-22	$594,000
2001	Bay Hill Invitational	-15	$630,000
2001	The Players Championship	-14	$1,080,000
2001	The Masters	-16	$1,008,000

Where to Write
Tiger Woods

Mr. Tiger Woods
c/o Professional Golfer's
Association of America
100 Avenue of the Champions
Box 109601
Palm Beach Gardens, FL 33410-9601

On the Internet at:

http://www.tigerwoods.com
http://espn.go.com/golfonline/profiles/tiger_woods.html
http://www.pga.com/

Index